SUPER BOWL
SUPER QUARTERBACKS

by JOE LAYDEN

SCHOLASTIC INC.

New York   Toronto   London   Auckland   Sydney
Mexico City   New Delhi   Hong Kong   Buenos Aires

ISBN 0-439-78433-6

12 11 10 9 8 7 6 5 4 3 2 1   5 6 7 8 9/0

Designed by Michael Malone
Printed in the U.S.A.
First printing, August 2005

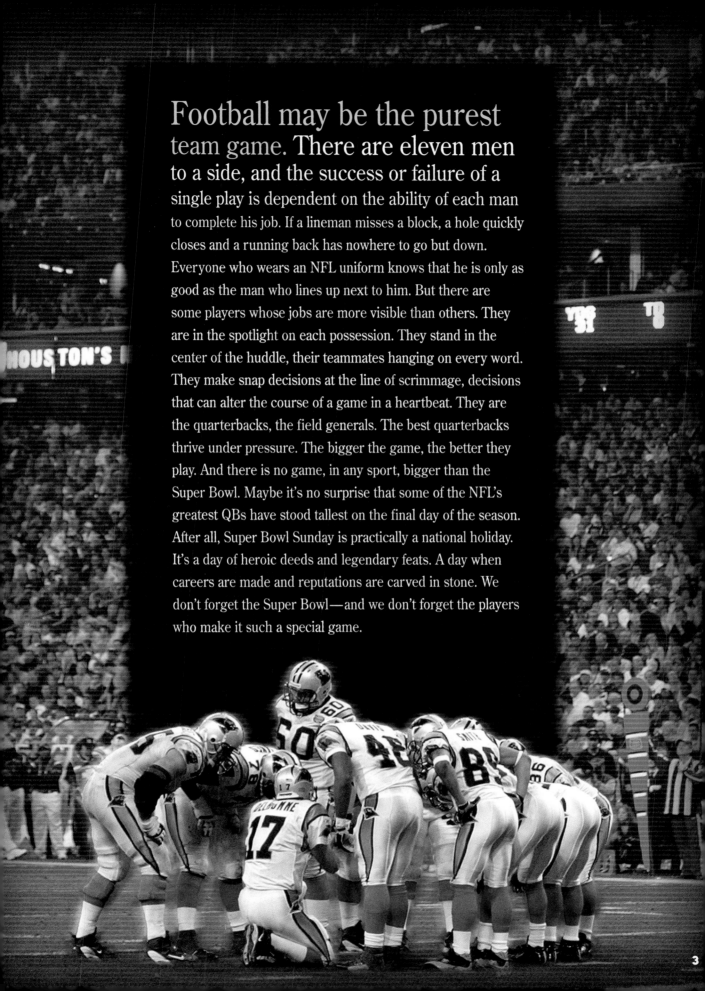

Football may be the purest team game. There are eleven men to a side, and the success or failure of a single play is dependent on the ability of each man to complete his job. If a lineman misses a block, a hole quickly closes and a running back has nowhere to go but down. Everyone who wears an NFL uniform knows that he is only as good as the man who lines up next to him. But there are some players whose jobs are more visible than others. They are in the spotlight on each possession. They stand in the center of the huddle, their teammates hanging on every word. They make snap decisions at the line of scrimmage, decisions that can alter the course of a game in a heartbeat. They are the quarterbacks, the field generals. The best quarterbacks thrive under pressure. The bigger the game, the better they play. And there is no game, in any sport, bigger than the Super Bowl. Maybe it's no surprise that some of the NFL's greatest QBs have stood tallest on the final day of the season. After all, Super Bowl Sunday is practically a national holiday. It's a day of heroic deeds and legendary feats. A day when careers are made and reputations are carved in stone. We don't forget the Super Bowl—and we don't forget the players who make it such a special game.

With a zealous fan base that seems to blanket the country, the Dallas Cowboys are affectionately known as America's Team. Never was this proud franchise more deserving of that nickname than in the mid-1990s, when they captured three Super Bowl titles in a span of just four years. That version of the Cowboys was one of the most dominant teams in NFL history. There were

THE GOLDEN BOY WAS ONE TOUGH COWBOY

many reasons for their success: the brilliant coaching of Jimmy Johnson, the dazzling, game-breaking running of Emmitt Smith, and a relentless, overwhelming defense. But if you want to find the root of the Cowboys' success, look no further than No. 8: quarterback Troy Aikman. On January 31, 1993, four years after Dallas made him the top pick in the NFL Draft, Troy delivered on his promise. In a stunning Super Bowl debut, he threw four touchdown passes and was named MVP, as the Cowboys defeated the Buffalo Bills, 52–17 for their first championship in fifteen years. Troy was a big, strong quarterback with the chiseled features of a movie star. But there was nothing soft or pampered about him. As his teammates were quick to point out, the golden boy was one tough Cowboy. He led Dallas to a second straight victory over the Bills in Super Bowl XXVIII, and a third title two years later, in Super Bowl XXX.

Emmitt Smith

Jimmy Johnson

Michael Irvin

		ATT	COM	YDS	TD	INT
SUPER BOWL XXVII	DAL 52, BUF 17	30	22	273	4	0
SUPER BOWL XXVIII	DAL 30, BUF 13	27	19	207	0	1
SUPER BOWL XXX	DAL 27, PIT 17	23	15	209	1	0
	TOTAL	80	56	689	5	1

TERRY
BRADSHAW
PITTSBURGH STEELERS

IX
X
XIII
XIV

When you think of the Pittsburgh Steelers and the great teams they fielded in the 1970s, you don't necessarily think of Terry Bradshaw. **This was a franchise defined** primarily by its vaunted "Steel Curtain" defense, one of the stingiest in NFL history. On offense, the Steelers employed a simple game plan: keep the ball on the ground and pass only when necessary. Fortunately, Terry was the perfect quarterback for this system. A fierce

THE BIGGER THE GAME THE BETTER HE WAS

competitor and field leader, he was one of the most efficient quarterbacks in the game. And the bigger the game, the better he was! Terry passed for more than 300 yards only seven times in his entire career. But three of those performances came in the playoffs. Two were in the Super Bowl. Terry acquired his first two rings in Super Bowls IX and X. In each of those games defense won the day for the Steelers. A few years later, though, the Steelers ran into a pair of teams that knew how to put points on the board, and Terry responded with two of the greatest performances of his career. He threw four touchdown passes in Super Bowl XIII as Pittsburgh defeated the Dallas Cowboys, 35–31. A year later, on January 20, 1980, the Steelers beat the Los Angeles Rams by a score of 31–19 for their fourth Super Bowl title. Once again Terry put on a breathtaking aerial show. He passed for 309 yards and two touchdowns as the Steelers officially earned the title "dynasty." Terry Bradshaw became the first quarterback to earn four Super Bowl rings. He also earned a spot in the Pro Football Hall of Fame.

Lynn Swann

"Mean" Joe Greene

		ATT	COM	YDS	TD	INT
SUPER BOWL IX	PIT 16, MIN 6	14	9	96	1	0
SUPER BOWL X	PIT 21, DAL 17	19	9	209	2	0
SUPER BOWL XIII	PIT 35, DAL 31	30	17	318	4	1
SUPER BOWL XIV	PIT 31, LA 19	21	14	309	2	3
	TOTAL	84	49	932	9	4

TOM
BRADY
NEW ENGLAND PATRIOTS

XXXVI
XXVIII
XXXIX

8

Tom Brady is not a screamer. You won't find him jumping around, pumping his fists, or giving a pep talk in the huddle. He is a natural leader, a man whose quiet confidence is contagious, which is why the New England Patriots have become

OTHER PLAYERS RALLY AROUND TOM

a dynasty in the new millennium. Other players rally around Tom. They look to him for guidance and inspiration, and he never lets them down. Just how good is Tom? Well, consider this: he already has three Super Bowl rings and two Super Bowl MVP trophies. That places him among the most successful quarterbacks in NFL history. The scary part is that Tom is only 27 years old! He has been in the league for just six years. It takes most quarterbacks that long just to learn the position. Not Tom. In 2002 he led the Patriots to a 20–17 victory over the St. Louis Rams and became the youngest quarterback to win a Super Bowl. If Tom was nervous before that game, you would never know it. Thirty minutes before kickoff he even took a nap! Two years later the Pats were back in the Super Bowl, and once again Tom was the star of the show. He threw three touchdown passes and was named MVP in a 32–29 victory over the Carolina Panthers. Tom picked up his third ring on February 6, 2005, when the Patriots beat the Philadelphia Eagles. As usual, Tom was nearly flawless. He completed 23 of 33 passes for 236 yards and two TDs. He did not pick up a third MVP trophy, but that's all right. It's the ring that counts.

Tedy Bruschi

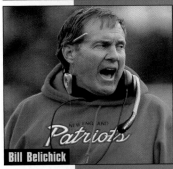
Bill Belichick

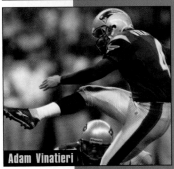
Adam Vinatieri

		ATT	COM	YDS	TD	INT
SUPER BOWL XXXVI	NE 20, STL 17	27	16	145	1	0
SUPER BOWL XXXVIII	NE 32, CAR 29	48	32	354	3	1
SUPER BOWL XXXIX	NE 24, PHL 21	33	23	236	2	0
	TOTAL	**108**	**71**	**735**	**6**	**1**

JOHN
ELWAY
DENVER BRONCOS

XXI
XXII
XXIV
XXXII
XXXIII

Flashback: a January night in 1998. The Denver Broncos have the ball on the 12-yard line of the Green Bay Packers in Super Bowl XXXII. Quarterback John Elway drops back to pass. Suddenly he's chased out of the pocket. John has been here before. In fact, this is his fourth Super Bowl appearance. So far, he has yet to emerge victorious. This time, though, John refuses to let the Broncos lose. While diving for the first down

JOHN PLAYS WITH THE BOUNDLESS ENERGY OF A KID

marker he is hit by several Green Bay defenders. His body twirls like a propeller in the air. But John hangs on to the ball and gets the first down! He rises from the pile and pumps a fist. The Broncos rally behind their quarterback to upset the Packers and capture their first Super Bowl title. But not their last. Denver returns to the Super Bowl one year later. And once again they ride the arm of their quarterback to victory. John will be remembered as one of the game's toughest competitors, and on this night he is at his best. In the final game of his long and illustrious career, at 38 years of age, John plays with the boundless energy of a kid. He throws for one touchdown and runs for another as the Broncos overpower the Atlanta Falcons by a score of 34–19. John is named MVP. It is the perfect ending for a man who will be remembered as one of the Super Bowl's greatest QBs.

Terrell Davis

Shannon Sharpe

		ATT	COM	YDS	TD	INT
SUPER BOWL XXI	NYG 39, DEN 20	37	22	304	1	1
SUPER BOWL XXII	WSH 42, DEN 10	38	14	257	1	3
SUPER BOWL XXIV	SF 55, DEN 10	26	10	108	0	2
SUPER BOWL XXXII	DEN 31, GB 24	22	12	123	0	1
SUPER BOWL XXXIII	DEN 34, ATL 19	29	18	336	1	1
	TOTAL	152	76	1,128	3	8

BRETT
FAVRE
GREEN BAY PACKERS

XXXI
XXXII

Born and raised in the deep South, Brett Favre quickly found a new home in one of the NFL's northernmost cities. If the cold, harsh winters of Wisconsin bothered him, you never knew it. With a strong arm and a ferociously competitive atti-

THE PACKERS BUILT THEIR OFFENSE AROUND HIM

tude, the kid from Southern Mississippi was precisely the right person to lead the Green Bay Packers back to respectability. By the time Brett arrived, the franchise had fallen on hard times. Not since

Reggie White

Dorsey Levens

Vince Lombardi and the glory days of the 1960s had anyone brought a title to Green Bay. That all changed when Brett took over at quarterback. The Packers built their offense around him, and Brett responded by breaking statistical records and winning awards. He was named the league's MVP for three consecutive seasons. But he wanted more than individual honors. Brett wanted a Super Bowl ring! On January 26, 1997, he finally got one. Brett was an all-purpose performer that day, throwing two touchdown passes and running for another as the Packers defeated the New England Patriots, 35–21, in Super Bowl XXXI. One year later, the Pack was back. In Super Bowl XXXII, only a touchdown by the Denver Broncos in the final two minutes prevented Green Bay from winning a second straight title. Brett threw three more touchdown passes in that game. Once again, the future Hall of Famer was nothing short of super.

	ATT	COM	YDS	TD	INT
SUPER BOWL XXXI GB 35, NE 21	27	14	246	2	0
SUPER BOWL XXXII DEN 31, GB 24	42	25	256	3	1
TOTAL	65	39	502	5	1

JOE
MONTANA
SAN FRANCISCO 49ERS

XVI
XIX
XXIII
XXIV

Back in 1979, when Joe Montana was a senior at Notre Dame, few people predicted that he would one day become the most successful quarterback in NFL history. Even the San Francisco 49ers had doubts—they did not select Joe until the third round of the NFL Draft. But within a couple years he had developed beyond anyone's expectations. Joe had a good arm, but that was not what made him special. Rather than drop back and patiently wait for a receiver to get open, Joe always seemed to be on the move. He routinely scrambled out of the pocket. And once he was loose, Joe was at his most dangerous. Sometimes he would run the ball. More often he would use his mobility to create chaos. Defenses never knew what to expect from Joe. Just when it looked like he was about to be sacked, he would avoid a tackle and unleash a perfect pass. Joe was

DEFENSES NEVER KNEW WHAT TO EXPECT FROM JOE

Jerry Rice

at his best on Super Bowl Sunday. The first of his three MVP awards came on January 24, 1982, in a 26–21 victory over the Cincinnati Bengals in Super Bowl XVI. He added another MVP award in Super Bowl XIX and a third in Super Bowl XXIV. In that game, a 55–10 rout of the Broncos, Joe threw a record five touchdown passes. But perhaps his best game was the one in which he was not named MVP: Super Bowl XXIII, in 1989. Displaying incredible confidence and poise, Joe led the 49ers on a 92-yard scoring drive in the final minute to defeat the Bengals, 20–16. Four rings and three MVP awards. It does not get much better than that.

		ATT	COM	YDS	TD	INT
SUPER BOWL XVI	SF 26, CIN 21	22	14	157	1	0
SUPER BOWL XIX	SF 38, MIA 16	35	24	331	3	0
SUPER BOWL XXIII	SF 20, CIN 16	36	23	357	2	0
SUPER BOWL XXIV	SF 55, DEN 10	29	22	297	5	0
	TOTAL	**122**	**83**	**1,142**	**11**	**0**

He played in only one Super Bowl, in which he did not throw a single touchdown pass. Nevertheless, there is no denying that Joe Namath was the star of Super Bowl III, a game that marked a turning point in NFL history. The first two Super Bowls had been dominated by the Green Bay Packers, champions of the established National Football League. Then along came the Jets, upstart champs of the American Football League, led

HE HAD GUTS AND A GREAT ARM

by a brash young quarterback who wore flashy white shoes and had the nerve to predict victory. "Broadway Joe," as New York sportswriters dubbed Namath, was actually a fairly conservative quarterback. He was smart and steady. He liked to step up into the pocket and find the open receiver. Slow-footed and cursed with bad knees, Joe was hardly a scrambler. But he had guts and a great arm. And both were on display in Miami, where the Jets faced Johnny Unitas and the Baltimore Colts in Super Bowl III. In the days leading up to the game, Joe had boldly declared that the Jets would beat the Colts. Most people laughed at him. After all, the Jets were huge underdogs. Joe did not care. On January 12, 1969, he led the Jets to a 16–7 victory over the Colts in one of the biggest Super Bowl upsets. Joe's performance was nearly flawless. But it was his leadership that meant the most. After the game he jogged off the field with a smile on his face and his index finger raised to the sky. Joe Namath and the Jets were No. 1!

Don Maynard

Johnny Unitas

	ATT	COM	YDS	TD	INT
SUPER BOWL III NYJ 16, BAL 7	28	17	206	0	0

PHIL
SIMMS
NEW YORK GIANTS

XXI

Phil Simms waited patiently for his chance to perform on football's biggest stage. A first-round draft pick in 1979, he was instantly declared a savior by long-suffering fans of the New York Giants. But the team's resurgence did not occur

ALWAYS THE PICTURE OF CALM AND CONTROL

overnight. It was not until the 1986 season that the Giants finally put it all together and won the NFC championship. In their first Super

Bowl appearance they routed the Denver Broncos, 39–20, at the Rose Bowl in Pasadena, California. On that evening, Phil Simms played the game of his life—and one of the greatest games ever recorded by a Super Bowl quarterback. Always the picture of calm and control, Phil was nothing less than masterful. He was also the game's MVP. Time after time, he dropped back in the pocket and ignored the charging defensive linemen of the Broncos. At the last second, just before getting tackled, Phil would release a perfect spiral that invariably found its way into the hands of the intended receiver. The Giants actually trailed by a score of 10–9 at halftime, but a 30-point outburst after the intermission buried the Broncos. Phil led the rally, of course. His 13-yard scoring strike to Mark Bavaro—always a favorite target—put the Giants ahead for good early in the third quarter. By game's end, Phil had thrown three touchdown passes; only three of his 25 passes fell incomplete. No quarterback in Super Bowl history has ever come so close to perfection. It was Phil's only appearance on Super Bowl Sunday, but he made certain it would be one to remember!

Mark Bavaro

Bill Parcells

	ATT	COM	YDS	TD	INT
SUPER BOWL XXI NYG 39, DEN 20	25	22	268	3	0

STEVE
YOUNG
SAN FRANCISCO 49ERS

XXIV
XXIX

24

There were times when Steve Young must have wondered whether he would ever get a chance to show what he could do. After all, it is not easy to be a backup behind one of the NFL's all-time great quarterbacks. But that was the challenge Steve faced. The first few years of his career were spent on the sideline, watching Joe Montana guide the 49ers to one championship after another.

STEVE'S GREATEST WEAPON WAS HIS ATHLETICISM

Once in a while he would mop up in a lopsided game, or fill in when Joe got hurt. It was not until January 29, 1995, at the age of 33, that Steve became a first-string Super Bowl quarterback. And what a performance it was! The crowd at Joe Robbie Stadium in Miami looked on in awe as Steve shredded the defense of the San Diego Chargers in Super Bowl XXIX. Steve's greatest weapon was his athleticism. He had a terrific arm, but he also had the ability to scramble out of trouble before passing, or even run with the ball when necessary. The Chargers chased Steve all over the field, but never could track him down. He threw a record six touchdown passes, including three to wide receiver Jerry Rice, as the 49ers cruised to their fifth NFL title with a 49–26 victory. When the game ended, Steve emerged from the long shadow of Joe Montana and accepted the MVP trophy. His place in NFL history was secure.

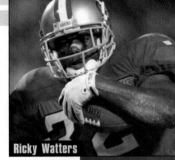
Ricky Watters

George Seifert

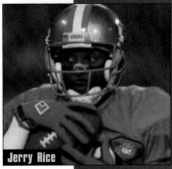
Jerry Rice

		ATT	COM	YDS	TD	INT
SUPER BOWL XXIV	SF 55, DEN 10	3	2	20	0	0
SUPER BOWL XXIX	SF 49, SD 26	36	24	325	6	0
	TOTAL	39	26	345	6	0

THE ROAD TO FORTY

JANUARY 15, 1967
Green Bay Packers 35, Kansas City Chiefs 10
MVP: Bart Starr, QB, Packers

JANUARY 14, 1968
Green Bay Packers 33, Oakland Raiders 14
MVP: Bart Starr, QB, Packers

JANUARY 12, 1969
New York Jets 16, Baltimore Colts 7
MVP: Joe Namath, QB, Jets

JANUARY 11, 1970
Kansas City Chiefs 23, Minnesota Vikings 7
MVP: Len Dawson, QB, Chiefs

JANUARY 17, 1971
Baltimore Colts 16, Dallas Cowboys 13
MVP: Chuck Howley, LB, Cowboys

JANUARY 16, 1972
Dallas Cowboys 24, Miami Dolphins 3
MVP: Roger Staubach, QB, Cowboys

JANUARY 14, 1973
Miami Dolphins 14, Washington Redskins 7
MVP: Jake Scott, S, Dolphins

JANUARY 13, 1974
Miami Dolphins 24, Minnesota Vikings 7
MVP: Larry Csonka, RB, Dolphins

JANUARY 12, 1975
Pittsburgh Steelers 16, Minnesota Vikings 6
MVP: Franco Harris, RB, Steelers

JANUARY 18, 1976
Pittsburgh Steelers 21, Dallas Cowboys 17
MVP: Lynn Swann, WR, Steelers

JANUARY 9, 1977
Oakland Raiders 32, Minnesota Vikings 14
MVP: Fred Biletnikoff, WR, Raiders

JANUARY 15, 1978
Dallas Cowboys 27, Denver Broncos 10
MVPs: Randy White, DT, Cowboys;
Harvey Martin, DE, Cowboys

JANUARY 21, 1979
Pittsburgh Steelers 35, Dallas Cowboys 31
MVP: Terry Bradshaw, QB, Steelers

JANUARY 20, 1980
Pittsburgh Steelers 31, Los Angeles Rams 19
MVP: Terry Bradshaw, QB, Steelers

JANUARY 25, 1981
Oakland Raiders 27, Philadelphia Eagles 10
MVP: Jim Plunkett, QB, Raiders

JANUARY 24, 1982
San Francisco 49ers 26, Cincinnati Bengals 21
MVP: Joe Montana, QB, 49ers

JANUARY 30, 1983
Washington Redskins 27, Miami Dolphins 17
MVP: John Riggins, RB, Redskins

JANUARY 22, 1984
Los Angeles Raiders 38, Washington Redskins 9
MVP: Marcus Allen, RB, Raiders

JANUARY 20, 1985
San Francisco 49ers 38, Miami Dolphins 16
MVP: Joe Montana, QB, 49ers

JANUARY 26, 1986
Chicago Bears 46, New England Patriots 10
MVP: Richard Dent, DE, Bears

JANUARY 25, 1987
New York Giants 39, Denver Broncos 20
MVP: Phil Simms, QB, Giants

JANUARY 31, 1988
Washington Redskins 42, Denver Broncos 10
MVP: Doug Williams, QB, Redskins

JANUARY 22, 1989
San Francisco 49ers 20, Cincinnati Bengals 16
MVP: Jerry Rice, WR, 49ers

JANUARY 28, 1990
San Francisco 49ers 55, Denver Broncos 10
MVP: Joe Montana, QB, 49ers

JANUARY 27, 1991
New York Giants 20, Buffalo Bills 19
MVP: Ottis Anderson, RB, Giants

JANUARY 26, 1992
Washington Redskins 37, Buffalo Bills 24
MVP: Mark Rypien, QB, Redskins

JANUARY 31, 1993
Dallas Cowboys 52, Buffalo Bills 17
MVP: Troy Aikman, QB, Cowboys

JANUARY 30, 1994
Dallas Cowboys 30, Buffalo Bills 13
MVP: Emmitt Smith, RB, Cowboys

JANUARY 29, 1995
San Francisco 49ers 49, San Diego Chargers 26
MVP: Steve Young, QB, 49ers

JANUARY 28, 1996
Dallas Cowboys 27, Pittsburgh Steelers 17
MVP: Larry Brown, CB, Cowboys

JANUARY 26, 1997
Green Bay Packers 35, New England Patriots 21
MVP: Desmond Howard, KR, Packers

JANUARY 25, 1998
Denver Broncos 31, Green Bay Packers 24
MVP: Terrell Davis, RB, Broncos

JANUARY 31, 1999
Denver Broncos 34, Atlanta Falcons 19
MVP: John Elway, QB, Broncos

JANUARY 30, 2000
St. Louis Rams 23, Tennessee Titans 16
MVP: Kurt Warner, QB, Rams

JANUARY 28, 2001
Baltimore Ravens 34, New York Giants 7
MVP: Ray Lewis, LB, Ravens

FEBRUARY 3, 2002
New England Patriots 20, St. Louis Rams 17
MVP: Tom Brady, QB, Patriots

JANUARY 26, 2003
Tampa Bay Buccaneers 48, Oakland Raiders 21
MVP: Dexter Jackson, S, Buccaneers

FEBRUARY 1, 2004
New England Patriots 32, Carolina Panthers 29
MVP: Tom Brady, QB, Patriots

FEBRUARY 6, 2005
New England Patriots 24, Philadelphia Eagles 21
MVP: Deion Branch, WR, Patriots

| PATRIOTS | 0 | 7 | 7 | 10 | 24 |
| EAGLES | 0 | 7 | 7 | 7 | 21 |

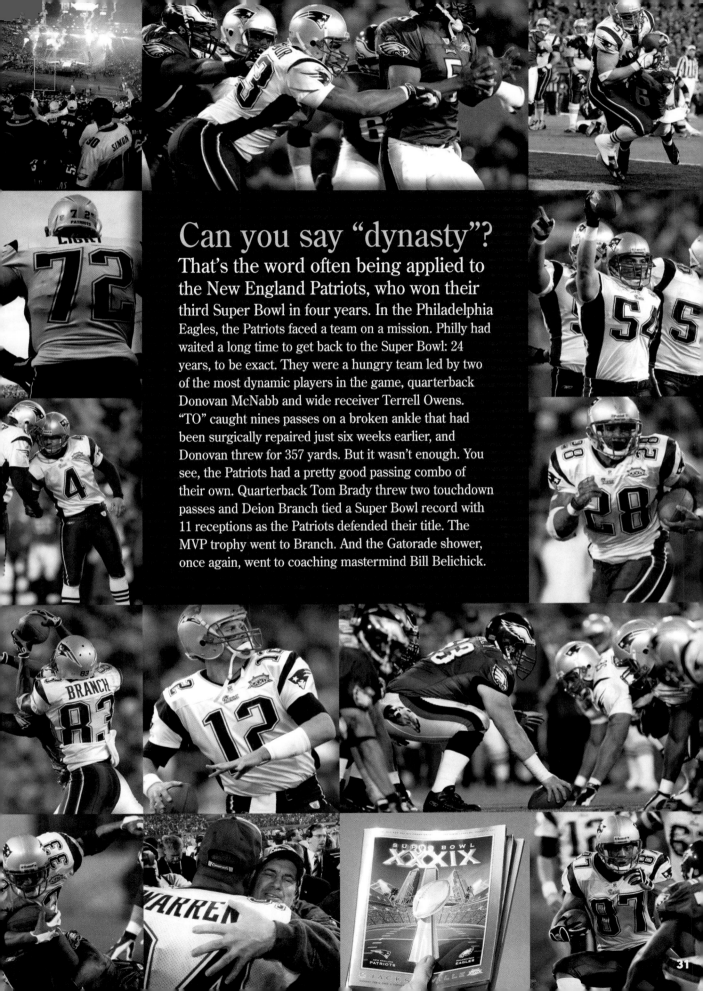

Can you say "dynasty"?

That's the word often being applied to the New England Patriots, who won their third Super Bowl in four years. In the Philadelphia Eagles, the Patriots faced a team on a mission. Philly had waited a long time to get back to the Super Bowl: 24 years, to be exact. They were a hungry team led by two of the most dynamic players in the game, quarterback Donovan McNabb and wide receiver Terrell Owens. "TO" caught nines passes on a broken ankle that had been surgically repaired just six weeks earlier, and Donovan threw for 357 yards. But it wasn't enough. You see, the Patriots had a pretty good passing combo of their own. Quarterback Tom Brady threw two touchdown passes and Deion Branch tied a Super Bowl record with 11 receptions as the Patriots defended their title. The MVP trophy went to Branch. And the Gatorade shower, once again, went to coaching mastermind Bill Belichick.

TOUCHDOWNS

3 **Roger Craig,** San Francisco, XIX
Jerry Rice, San Francisco, XXIV
Ricky Watters, San Francisco, XXIX
Terrell Davis, Denver, XXXII

FIELD GOALS

3 **Don Chandler,** Green Bay, II
Ray Wersching, San Francisco, XVI

LONGEST FIELD GOAL

54 **Steve Christie,** Buffalo, XXVIII

RUSHING YARDS

204 **Timmy Smith,** Washington, XXII
191 **Marcus Allen,** L.A. Raiders, XVIII
166 **John Riggins,** Washington, XVII

LONGEST RUN FROM SCRIMMAGE

74 **Marcus Allen,** L.A. Raiders, XVIII

RUSHING TOUCHDOWNS

3 **Terrell Davis,** Denver, XXXII

HIGHEST COMPLETION PERCENTAGE

88.0 **Phil Simms,** New York Giants, XXI
75.9 **Joe Montana,** San Francisco, XXIV
73.5 **Ken Anderson,** Cincinnati, XVI

TOUCHDOWN PASSES

6 **Steve Young,** San Francisco, XXIX

PASSING YARDS

414 **Kurt Warner,** St. Louis, XXXIV
365 **Kurt Warner,** St. Louis, XXXVI
357 **Joe Montana,** San Francisco, XXIII
357 **Donovan McNabb,** Philadelphia, XXXIX

LONGEST PASS COMPLETION

85 **Jake Delhomme (to Muhsin Muhammad),** Carolina, XXXVIII

RECEPTIONS

11 **Dan Ross,** Cincinnati, XVI
Jerry Rice, San Francisco, XXIII
Deion Branch, New England, XXXIX

RECEIVING YARDS

215 **Jerry Rice,** San Francisco, XXIII
193 **Ricky Sanders,** Washington, XXII
162 **Isaac Bruce,** St. Louis, XXXIV

SACKS

3 **Reggie White,** Green Bay, XXXI

DATE DUE

JUL 1 0 2006	WITHDRAWN
SEP 2 6 2006	
OCT 1 2 2006	
JAN 0 8 2007	
AUG 2 1 2007	WITHDRAWN
OCT 9 2007	
NOV 1 3 2007	
FEB 9 2008	
SEP 1 2009	
OCT 5 2010	
OCT 2 2 2012	WITHDRAWN
FEB 1 5 2013	
DEC 1 0 2014	
NOV 2 2 2016	